The double soul of the United States:

The Democratic Party is given over to satan

Enrique de Diego

Foreword by Mike Sala

Prologue: The Struggle of Good against Evil

The arrival of the Pilgrims on the shores of Massachusetts in 1620, after a perilous voyage of two months and five days from Plymouth, marked the beginning of a crucial and hugely important era in human history.

Those little more than a hundred pioneer pilgrims, who left Europe in search of a land in New England where they could settle in freedom of conscience and worship, seeking spiritual and material prosperity under the guidance of God through the Bible, were the seed of a nation that, with many lights and no less shadows, would end up being a definitive reference not only for what we usually call the West, but also, in one way or another, for practically all the nations of the world.

But what is it that has given the United States its eminent place in today's civilisation? Precisely the principles under which they were founded as a nation after the war of independence against the British crown. While the European nations lived under the yoke of absolutist and dictatorial monarchies and political and religious institutions, those first thirteen overseas colonies were strengthening a libertarian spirit that would eventually crystallise in the federal nation that emerged after the achievement of their independence. Over time, despite continued attempts by the powers that be to pervert the founding principles of the US Constitution, a large part of the American people, certainly in some states more than others, have preserved the "American spirit" way of life which means that even today, in the midst of unprecedented and threatening social and political upheaval, the United States remains a land of freedom and opportunity.

During the last two years of planned globalist social engineering by the elites, a significant part of the American people have displayed the libertarian spirit that nestles in their hearts. The overturning of the satanic Roe Vs Wade abortion ruling, the relentless struggle against the degenerate movements and associations that seek to sexually pervert children and young people from the very beginning of their lives, the determination to stand up to the gangs of looters who find ideological refuge in fascistic racialist and communist movements akin to the Democratic Party, the resistance to the power that seeks to take away the people's firearms and capacity for self-defence, the resistance to the Covid tyranny whose deadly outcome is plain for all to see, and the exposure of the fallacy of climate change, have been far more profound than in other nations.

whose peoples have also resisted such attacks on truth and freedom. In America there is Christian and moral reserve, generally located in those states that make up the "Bible Belt" and the "Mormon Corridor", along with other states of republican and conservative Christian tradition, several of them located in the Midwest. Such a phenomenon is not found in any other Western nation, where there may also be resistance but with little of the faith base and individual freedom necessary to orchestrate a spontaneous national and spiritual sentiment so compact as to successfully oppose the aforementioned manoeuvres that make up the globalist agenda's strategy of domination and extermination. The United States is the best and worst example of all of the above. It is the nation where immensely powerful elites work for Evil. It is the nation where religious denominations, communities and states rise up as one to defend and preserve the Good. It is the nation with a double soul.

This book by Enrique de Diego is much more than a quick review of US history and a brief analysis of a series of current events that are absolutely important for our present and future. **The Double Soul of the United States** is an apt exposition that will make the reader reflect on what has been happening over the past decades and how the different master lines of the globalist agenda converge towards the same end, which is the domination and extermination of a large part of the world's population in favour of the elites who dominate the political, religious and social spheres of the vast majority of nations.

America's double soul comes at a most opportune moment. Just a few years ago, when hardly anyone considered the existence of great powers whose intentions were to ruin health, the economy, morality and any other right principle that could help build decent and just societies, this book would have been labelled "conspiratorial" not only by the media, journalists, communicators and any other servants of the system; a majority of readers would also have labelled the author a madman.

Today, however, with the perspective gained after a plandemic designed to lead the world into the abyss, with a devastating economic crisis looming, with a war unleashed on Europe's doorstep by the same people responsible for killing millions during the past nightmare years Covid, with the imposition of ideologies that particularly attack the family, life and the integrity of born and unborn children, adolescents and the elderly, with the deception of climate change turned into doctrine and with an iron censorship that tries to keep the population ignorant, books such as **The Double Soul of**

The United States makes sense and coherence. The danger looming over our societies and way of life is real and with each passing day shows its abject face more clearly. The dark aims of the globalist agenda driven by so-called philanthropists, and by religious, social and economic powers infiltrated by Satanism, seek nothing more than to alienate human beings in the most nefarious way and with the most terrible consequences humanity has ever experienced. We are in a total war between the elites and the people all over the world. Everything seems to be rushing before our eyes. The globalist agenda no longer gives us any respite between one planned tragedy and the next. But many of the people resist. That is why the elites of the globalist agenda understand that strongholds like the United States must be attacked more fiercely and on all possible fronts. The elites know that if the US falls, the rest of the resistance will fall too. This and no other is the reason for the continued attack and war unleashed across that nation for decades, and Enrique de Diego's **The Double Soul of the United States** will help the reader to better understand the magnitude of the current moment we are living through.

Mike Sala

Between religion and greed

"This soil has grown so weary of its inhabitants that man, the most precious of all creatures, is here more vile and abject than the earth he treads upon. We have reached the highest degree of intemperance by cultivating all sorts of excesses. The sources of knowledge and religion have been corrupted. Most of the children, even the most intelligent and those from whom the most can be expected, are perverted, corrupted, and deeply overwhelmed by the multitude of bad examples and the licentious government of their schools".

This diagnosis of the United States could be predicated on the once Fatherland of Liberty and its deep and intense decadence, but its author is John Winthrop and it is found in his General Observations for the Plantation of New England. John Winthrop was the moral leader of the Puritans on the Mayflower, an old freighter that used to carry barrels of claret wine from Bordeaux to London and had been leased by a group of English Calvinists. And it was John Winthrop who organised and commanded in 1630 the largest contingent called upon to found a new colony that would eventually become the United States of America.

After many vicissitudes and various expeditions marked by greed, which were shipwrecked in failure or piracy, giving rise to the disappeared colony of Roanoke, which is lost in mystery, exterminated by the Indians, it was the religious impulse that gave the strength and constancy to lay firm foundations for the embryo of what would later become a great nation. Religious nonconformists, fleeing the corruption of the Church of England, were the founders of what John Winthrop summed up in a startling and visionary phrase, like a new Moses in Exodus: "we must consider that we shall be as a city upon a hill, the eyes of the whole world are upon us".

John Harvard

They were not illiterate but sought from the first to ensure the education of their offspring, training them in evangelical orthodoxy and the moral principles of the Bible. That was the sense in which, in 1636, the Reverend John Harvard made his testamentary bequest, which gave rise to the famous University, far removed from its founding principles: to provide a levy of well-trained clergymen. And that was also the meaning of the founding of Yale by Elihu Yale, a scholar from a saga of pious Puritans who had emigrated from Boston because he considered it to be corrupt.

Almost a century later, another Puritan, Cotton Mather recognised that time had worked against him and that the religion the Puritans had brought to America was changing beyond recognition. In 1702, he published his most important work, Magnalia Christi America, in which he declared that "religion gave birth to prosperity, and the daughter destroyed the mother". A remarkable distinction, for let us not forget that the Puritans were Calvinists and considered that in the just the attainment of earthly goods, the fruit of their work and effort, were a manifestation of God's predilection.

It was not a difference between prosperity and religion, therefore, but between the accumulation of goods without ethics, without natural order. That dichotomy has only grown and opened a gulf in an increasingly polarised America; or between an America, that city on the hill, which lives by the ten commandments and in which the Word of God and the natural order governs their lives and they tend to be libertarians, ready to defend their freedom and the security of their home and the tranquillity of their community with arms; and an amorphous entity, of globalist tendency, which considers man autonomous of all moral standards, post-Christian, diverse, trans, indoctrinating, slave-owning, abortionist, Malthusian, which has gone by unrestricted lying to the point of infamous genocide with vaccine scams. The two United States cannot coexist. It is not a dual society, for one side has disavowed the founding principles and hates them, dreaming dystopian dreams of a world government. It is a confrontational and conflicted society on the verge of exploding and it is good that it is exploding.

But let us not get ahead of ourselves. That atmosphere of the Pilgrim Fathers, and to a large extent of the Founding Fathers, reemerged with a vengeance in the West of the wagons and the duels. It was the Great Awakening. Around 1740 there was a generation of itinerant preachers who travelled the frontiers preaching to the lowly, a spiritual movement of enormous scope, emotionally preparing Americans for the Revolution and Independence. Patriotism merged with non-denominational Christianity and liberty. The First Amendment specifically rejects the establishment of a national church and prohibits Congress from passing "any law respecting an establishment of religion, or prohibiting the free exercise thereof".

The Second Great Awakening, which began in the 1790s and developed again on the frontier, was carried out by travelling evangelists who held mass meetings in the open air. In this environment were born the Adventists and the Church of Jesus Christ or Latter-day Saints, known as the Mormons, who after an epic exodus across plains and mountains between 1846 and 1847, arrived in Salt Lake City and gave birth to the state of Utah, which has been one of the wealthiest, best educated and most observant of the Law.

Thus the Midwest, the prairie region and the Rocky Mountains were formed as the states of libertarian spirit and faith in God and country; the so-called Bible Circle. Opposite were the intellectuals of the East Coast and Sin City, which, by a strange irony, is called San Francisco. Both have had a dialectic of confrontation, the one of the intellectuals has underestimated the other, has placed itself in a position of indoctrination, but they seemed to be the opposing forces of a great nation, until the one of the coasts, the one of the elites, the one of the elite Universities and Silicon Valley decided to subdue the other, and in full sense exterminate it, using as an instrument a corrupt Democratic Party, and a good part of the Republican Party, producing an inversion of common sense, breaking social cohesion for the sake of diversity, and of moral sense by corrupting children through indoctrination in school, in every moral disorder is promoted.

The two United States were shaped in the concrete rule of law and in the republic, in the government for the people, by the people, of the people, of Jefferson and Abraham Lincoln, but the democrat party decided to provoke, within its totalitarian and genocidal drive, a colossal electoral fraud in the 2020 elections, and to impose its agenda by means of mandates by an old fuddy-duddy with serious shortcomings and shortcomings, the dumbest and most corrupt they could find, and the United States, the real one, for the other is unrecognisable, has resisted the crazed and genocidal onslaught and is now going on the counter-offensive, in a regeneration of the nation and a moral rearmament.

From the hoax of evolutionism to social Darwinism

The United States, as the Homeland of Freedom, was configured around the melting pot, the melting pot, thus assimilating large numbers of immigrants, on three axes: English as a language, patriotism as concrete, symbolised by respect for the anthem and the flag, and Christianity. There is a clear moment when the two souls of America, or America in soul, bifurcate and drift apart. It was in the bitter controversy between creationism and evolutionism, or the way it should be taught in schools, as just another theory, a hypothesis, a rather fallacious one at that, or as dogma.

When a law went into effect in Tennessee prohibiting public school teachers from teaching Darwinian evolution to children, the American Civil Liberties Union sued. The Midwestern spokesman, William Jennings Bryan, and in droves the East Coast press and "intellectuals", readers of The Education of Henry Adams, a posthumous autobiography of the archetypal Boston mandarin, published in 1918 and until the early 1920s the most popular non-fiction book in the United States, clashed. It criticised "Americanisation" in favour of what Adams called "multidiversity". He criticised the melting pot because he understood that it was intended to make everyone Anglo-Saxon and that they should pursue "the more adventurous ideal" of cosmopolitanism (today we would say globalism) and become "the first international nation".

The arrogance of the "intellectuals" who considered that they had "a monopoly on the existing oxygen on the North American continent" was brought to bear on William Jennings Bryan by offering a caricature of him and his positions. It was one of the clearest operations of manipulation on a grand scale. Bryan, a Democrat from Illinois, a

A pacifist who had resigned as Secretary of State with America's entry into World War I, had fought for women's suffrage, and for all genuinely progressive causes, he was portrayed as a reactionary oaf when he tried to prevent evolutionism from being taught as dogma, not hypothesis, and religious teachings from being weakened, that parental rights should be addressed. Bryan won the trial but the press took it upon themselves to crucify him.

Darwinian evolutionism has been taught ever since as dogma, despite being an imaginative science fiction hoax, so that from amoeba to man, no one knows why, because there is no evidence for it in nature, no leaps in the creation of organs, and the latest hoax, of mutations taking thousands of years to occur, clashes with the evidence that all mutations are regressive and do not survive. This witch's tale has become the standard of the "intellectuals", the dogma of the schools, so that generations have learned to "believe" in evolution. A dictatorship was thus imposed in schools that has been growing as an attack on religion and all moral standards, replaced by a new religion, a new inquisition and new dogmas, made up of post-modern clichés, with very persistent secular anathemas, against everything that the United States has stood for.

At the time, the philosopher John Dewey could see that this would lead to the destruction of the nation, and in the face of the fatuous arrogance of his peers, he explained that Bryan was speaking for some of the best and most essential elements of American society, "the church-going classes, those who come under evangelical Christianity. These people are the backbone of philanthropic social interest, of social reform through political action, of pacifism, of popular education. They embody and express the spirit of cordial goodwill towards the economically disadvantaged classes and towards other nations, especially when these show some disposition to the republican form of government. The Middle West, the prairie region, has been the centre of active social philosophy and political progressivism; as they believe in education and better opportunities for their own children. They have been the very people who responded to calls for fair treatment and fuller equality of opportunity for all. They followed Lincoln in abolishing slavery and followed Roosevelt in his attack on 'evil' corporations and accumulations of wealth. He has been at the centre in every sense of the word and in every movement".

This ideological dictatorship came to the fore in the 1970s, when the Supreme Court in "Roe v. Wide" ruled (seven to two) that the option to choose an abortion during the first trimester of pregnancy was a fundamental constitutional privilege, implying, by a legal fallacy, that the laws of the states were null and void. This decision is to be reversed in a regenerative act, fundamental to the survival of the United States as a nation and to the survival of the species. Let us hope so.

In the 1990s, after the fall of the Berlin Wall, the elite universities began to militate with increasing fervour and superlative tyranny for relativism and decreed the arrival of post-modernity, nimbued with the disintegrating concept of diversity, inclusive language and gender ideology. The origin of the elimination of Marxism, which was already a relativism, was that since the dialectical materialism that claimed to be scientific had been demonstrated in false praxis, then truth had ceased to exist and we had entered postmodernity, where everything was valid and the old values of truth and lies were perished. Yavalism was enthroned as dogma and lies dominated as never before, moral disorder and transgression tried to impose themselves as the norm with a vicious intolerance and new sins, such as homophobia and systemic racism, took centre stage.

I remember a conversation with a friend of mine who was on a trip to the United States when he told me about the new semantic style, and I thought it was delirious. Now it has come to gender ideology run amok and the woke system. Christian and libertarian America is reacting. Because of the new and shocking nonsense, born in the elite universities, imposed by teachers imbued with the new destructive dogmas, the governor of Florida, Ron DeSantis has banned its dissemination in schools and in the face of the aggressive position of Disney has ended the privileges of autonomy in Orlando, which has represented a significant fall of the shares, a good part of which are owned by the bad George Soros. Netflix, which has bet on this delusion in a disgusting way, has collapsed and is just waiting for the coup de grâce. Christian America, which seemed to be asleep, has come out of its lethargy and has started the counter-offensive marked by success, with the conviction that the satanic goal is the corruption of children from their earliest childhood and the legalisation of the pederasty these degenerates dream of.

The latest episode, within the diabolical logic of social Darwinism, has been the lie of the vaccination scam; a genocidal deception which, according to Malthusian theses reissued under the fallacious impulse of the climate scam, is intended. The Christian and libertarian United States has courageously resisted and has not given in to the lie of Anthony Fauci and Bill Gates.

The proposal for the extermination of the white man, monopolist of original sin

Two United States live side by side in the same territory; one has reached a level of degeneracy that makes Sodom and Gomorrah look ridiculous, the other still has God, the Bible and the Fatherland at the centre of its life. The first one is extremely intolerant and tries to infect the other with its moral detritus and to overwhelm it with its half-baked dogmas and anathemas, which must be taken seriously in a hurry. The other defends the right to life, to private property, to liberty and to defend them with the right to bear arms; the other is obsessed with disarming you in order to impose its depraved criteria, which it displays with a false moral superiority. The one is no longer the United States, it is no longer the Homeland of Freedom, it abominates its founding principles in order to instigate a new world order, an atrocious tyranny built on leavings of the idle through welfarism.

This degenerate United States, which has its epicentres in California, which became the world's 5th economic power, in New York, in Massachusetts, Maryland, in the two coastal areas, has gone a step further and has tried to impose its delirious criteria, without any rational basis, in schools, which have been used for the indoctrination and moral corruption of children. With gender ideology, the proposal of universal sodomy has been overtaken by queer feminism and the trans movement, various forms of which aim to subvert the natural order of things, generate confusion about one's own sexuality and destroy the family and the birth rate.

This movement that has infected the Democratic Party, unrecognisable to its founder. Andrew Jackson, until it looks like a chaotic conglomerate of Luciferian ideas, in which there are the elites, what Ludwig von Mises called "Broadway communism", those who try to legitimise their fortune so easily obtained thanks to the market with their radical positions, as is the case of Leonardo Dicaprio.

But now his proposal is not to be taken as an occurrence, or a distortion of history and reality, but as a strict proposal for the extermination of the white, heterosexual, Christian man. The annihilationist theoretical basis is given the name of "critical race theory" and has its instrument in Black Lives Matter and its symbolism in the kneeling salute, ultimate humiliation. In a theological sense, what "critical race theory" preaches is the monopoly of original sin by the white man, so that his nature is corrupted, indelibly, unforgivably, the cause of all evils and has a "systemic racism" from which it cannot be shaken off. By contrast, all the ethnic minorities into which American society has been compartmentalised are devoid of original sin, angelic and propitiatory victims, against the evidence, of that evil which nests in the intrinsically evil white man, who must be exterminated or by dint of self-flagellation should resort to collective suicide.

In that kingdom of Satan that is California, which is sinking into the quagmire, where George Soros has sown tares in the hands of even the district attorneys, they seem more like friends of criminals than protectors of citizens' rights, especially when racial prejudice is involved.

Indeed, the United States had a very bloody civil war to eliminate slavery, which was practised by blacks, tribes against tribes, and Arabs, and which was considered normal, until various Christian tendencies opposed it and started the abolitionist movement. Abraham Lincoln was horrified that slavery would infect the entire Union and envisaged various actions to return the blacks to Africa, but all were failures. An expedition to the Dominican Republic garnered only 1,170 volunteers, as did contingents to Liberia, which no one will think to cite as a successful example. Whites shed their blood abundantly and generously in that struggle.

Today, with isolated cases struggling on merit, the black community has suffered a brutal deterioration in its moral standards. In 1960 the percentage of illegitimate children among blacks was 24%, in 1991 illegitimacy jumped to 68%. In some places, such as Washington, it was over 90%. Blacks as a community appear dedicated to welfarism, practised by the diabolical Democratic Party as vote-buying, and repugnant to the libertarian foundations of America, supposedly once a land of opportunity to make one's own way through hard work. Execrated from the melting pot, blacks have been clustering in their neighbourhoods, where the most egregious racism is practised, and where a white man cannot, at the risk of his life, go. The same is true of certain Latino communities, such as the welfare-oriented Puerto Ricans.

The genocidal danger that incubates the so-called "critical race theory" has begun to be fought tooth and nail by Florida Governor Ron DeSantis, who has banned it from schools and textbooks; an example that should be followed with the utmost urgency by most states that do not aspire to surpass Sodom and Gomorrah, out of sheer survival instinct. The ethnic replacement of the white race is hidden under the woke ideology, which should not be taken as a joke.

Luciferian ironies, colossal electoral fraud, Biden, the corrupt madman

Sometimes, Satan manifests himself through glorious ironies so that it is seen that he is the one who acts: Joe Biden, an abject character, a paedophile with gross accusations of his daughter performing improper acts with her, who cannot sit still when he sees a child but gropes him and is corrupt to the max, with his son Hunter, another despicable character, morally inferior, whose personal computer contains photos of paedophilia and signs of his high corruption in Ukraine, who was capable of sleeping with his dead brother's wife in the middle of a wake. The Biden's, a paragon of vices in the light of day, whose constant gaffes are whitewashed by the media, who refuse to investigate his blatant corruption and cover his ridiculousness with an ever thinner cloak.

It seems unbelievable how low the United States and the presidency have sunk. It was all because of a colossal electoral fraud. Donald Trump won, unexpectedly, over the satanic Hillary Clinton, the choice of the elites, a woman complacent with Bill, friend of Jeffrey Epstein, the suicidal paedophile. The media then conspired with the supposed masters of the world that Trump would be a stopgap, that he could not, in any case, win the election for a second term. Several states changed their electoral rules to facilitate fraud and hired the company Dominion, a Chavist offshoot specialising in fraud.

After a tenacious media opposition, which presented a successful Donald Trump in a parody of himself, with calls from the Democratic Party to vote by mail, in order to propitiate the rigging, with the polls shot in favour of a Joe Biden who in the election debates had to be picked up by the moderators, given his numerous hissy fits, when Trump dared to bring up the family corruption of his son Hunter, the most scandalous electoral fraud in history was brought about, involving both the poisonous sewer that the Democratic Party has degenerated into and the corruption of the Republican Party, in which the cases of the governors of Georgia and Wisconsin are under suspicion. All the counterpowers of the American political model failed miserably, to put the degenerate Biden in the White House.

Trump who well defined his enemies as the "deep state" and the "swamp", however, did little or nothing to defuse them. This is what happened with the genocidal Anthony Fauci, who, according to Dr. Vladimir Zelenko, and Oklahoma Republican Party chairman John Bennet, should be tried and immediately put before a firing squad, with the FDA and CDC executives. Biden showed what a clownish wimp he is by mandating criminal vaccination scams and inappropriate use of masks in a heinous masquerade, which he must pay for after a fair trial.

The elections on 11 November are shaping up to be the elections in which the Democratic Party and Joe Biden will pay for their electoral fraud and their puppet presidency. The Luciferian irony will come to an end.

Playing corrupting and paedophile social ingeria with our children

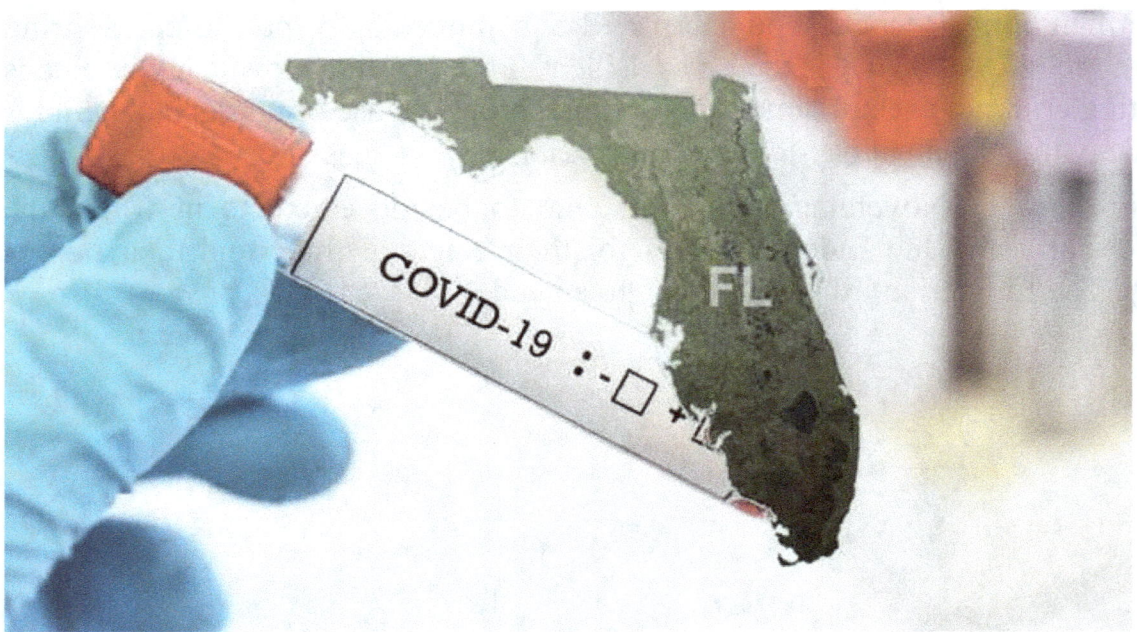

The double soul, one satanic and welfarist, conspiring for the extermination of the white man, has its paradigm in California; the other Christian, libertarian, melting pot, has its paradigm in Florida. California practices multidiversity, while Florida practices the melting pot. California became the fifth world power when Ronald Reagan was governor, but since then it has done nothing but decline. Florida, with no income tax, does nothing but flourish.

Gavin Newson, Governor of California.

California has two powerful industries given over to evil: Hollywood and Silicon Valey. All depravity has its seat there. Its governor Gabin Newson aspires to to turn that state into a "sanctuary" for abortion. Not only that: it intends to legalise infanticide, proceeding to the brutal murder of babies weeks, months or even years after they are born. Its legislators will consider a horrific bill. According to the text, a "person shall not be subject to civil or criminal liability or sanction, or otherwise deprived of his or her rights, on account of his or her actions or omissions with respect to his or her pregnancy or the actual, potential or presumed outcome of the pregnancy, including miscarriage, stillbirth, stillbirth, abortion or death. The term "fetal death, miscarriage, abortion or perinatal death" shall not apply.

A Northern California city has declared independence from the vaccine scam and facemasks mandates of President Biden and the governor. Northern California has a strong feeling for statehood. The people call themselves Oroville: "It is time for we, the people, to stand up against the overreach of these power-hungry radicalised politicians. Just because something makes sense in big cities like (San Francisco), (Los Angeles) or Sacramento doesn't mean it makes sense in rural Oroville. Sadly, our governor has not been willing or open to listen to the north state ... If he would just listen to their comments, we wouldn't be here".

San Francisco is a gay city without children. Far worse than Sodom and Gomorrah. Welfareism has been legitimised by the Democratic Party. The University of California has expelled professors for refusing to be injected. Genocide has been taken to its ultimate consequences and in Ventura County an exponential increase in heart, cerebrovascular and blood clotting problems has been detected.

In Florida, the majority of the population has not been vaccinated and the governor, Ron DeSantis, has refused to inject children. He has decided to ban indoctrination in schools. Several mothers protested that their children had been tried to be turned trans. Disney rejected this law and said it would fight it. Their plans included making 50% of the characters in their films sodomites. Ron DeSantis countered Disney's position by stripping Disney of all its privileges in Orlando, which has plunged the company into a deep crisis with continued stock market declines.

Floridians are not Anglo-Saxon but they respect the founding principles that made America great. They abhor welfarism and, as a result, have low taxes. It is a successful model. There is a saying that if you give a dollar to a Cuban American he thinks about where to invest it and where to open a business; if you give it to a Puerto Rican in New York he spends it quickly on alcohol or drugs.

California and Florida are the two polar opposites, the two souls of the United States. There is a long-standing tradition of migration between states in search of an environment conducive to decency and a sense of religion. This phenomenon has also been detected now. In the wake of the 2020 election fraud, emigration has begun.

towards Midwestern states, from the Bible Circle. Not only individual or family decisions, but also companies are looking for more family-friendly places for their workers and lower taxes for them. It is a phenomenon that is only increasing.

It is the flight, the exodus from states such as California or Maryland, where the legalisation of infanticide is also being considered, the end of which is glimpsed in the Mad Max film, amidst racial conflict, urban tribes and the most abject moral degeneration.

One part, the part that votes for the Democratic Party, has turned its back on God, has ceased to be America.

Half of the United States, or somewhat less, because in the year 2020 a monumental fraud took place, has turned its back on God, something unheard of in the history of that great nation, today an absolute parody of a first power, hysterical at the possibility of the Supreme Court returning to the States their ability to legislate on abortion. In that half, or something less, there is an escalation towards unrestricted depravity; abortion is presented as a matter of "reproductive health"; death for the baby, no health for the murderous woman; infanticide is already being flirted with; Afghanistan is leaving its tail between its legs, while Ukraine is living in the strictest hypocrisy and giving business to the military industrial complex. The United States is ready to defend values, but it does not know which values and certainly not its own, as a "city on the hill", as a Christian nation, although there are states, most of them, which consider the Gospel as their guide and Freedom as their north.

Benjamin Franklin, one of the Founding Fathers, wrote to Thomas Paine to reproach him for considering religion unnecessary: "He who spits at heaven spits at himself. If men have religion and are wicked, what would become of them if they had none? John Adams, who was the second president, wrote: "One of the great advantages of Christianity is that it makes all the people know, believe, and worship the great principle of the law of nature and nations, to love your neighbour as yourself, and not to do to others what you would not have them do to you.

On a memorable occasion, at the farewell of his second term and public life, George Washington, gave his political testament: "All the arrangements and habits which have made political prosperity possible have had the indispensable support of religion and morality". Anyone who sought to undermine "these firm supports of the duties of men and citizens" was the exact opposite of a patriot. It is impossible for there to be any kind of "security for property, for reputation, for life, if the sense of religious obligation does not accompany the oaths which are the investigative instrument of courts of justice".

Nor can morality be maintained without religion. However much help "refined education" alone might provide to "minds of a peculiar structure", experience showed that "national morality" could not be established "to the exclusion of the religious principle". In fact, Washington's point was that the United States, as a free republic whose order depended on the good behaviour of its citizens, could not survive without religion.

In the bloody Civil War, Abraham Lincoln, when asked if God was on the side of the North, replied: "That does not worry me at all, because I know that the Lord is always on the side of the good guys. What never ceases to distress me, what I constantly pray for, is that I, and this nation, may be on the Lord's side". And in his memorable inaugural address of his second term he said. "Both read the same Bible and pray to the same God, and each invokes His help against the other. It may seem strange that a man should dare to ask God's righteous help to earn his bread by the sweat of other men; but let us not judge if we do not want to be judged. The prayers of one or the other could not be answered; none have been fully answered. The Almighty has His own designs: 'Cursed be the world for offences committed! Offences are unavoidable, but woe to the man who commits them!' We hope - we earnestly pray - that this tremendous scourge of war will at last be brought to an end. If, however, God wills that it should continue until the wealth accumulated by the two hundred and fifty years of unrewarded toil of the slave man shall be exhausted, and until every drop shed by the lash shall be paid by every drop shed by the sword, as was said three thousand years ago, even then we must say that 'the judgment of God is always right and just.

America's destiny is intimately tied to God, to religion and to the moral order, to the natural law that is inscribed in every heart to distinguish right from wrong. One part of America is faithful to this legacy, but another part, the part that votes for the Democratic Party and worships its absurd theories, has turned away from God and is on the road to perdition. It has turned away from the same natural order through divorce, abortion, gender ideology, and now encourages the hope of complete depravity with paedophilia and infanticide. Sodom and Gomorrah overcome. Another America worships God, Life and Liberty, it is the circle of the Bible, the Mormon corridor with epicentre in the State of Utah, the Midwest with Texas and Oklahoma, and Florida. It is again the "city on the hill" to which all eyes turn. It seems that the part that has ceased to be America and the part that maintains, renewed, the principles of the Pilgrim Fathers and the Fathers of the nation, cannot coexist, for they are like oil and water. There must be a moral rearmament, a beneficial polarisation, without compromise or concession, because the future of civilisation and the species is at stake. And, as the Bible says, omne regnum divisum contra se, desolabitur. Every kingdom divided against itself will be desolate.

The legacy   from   Theodore   Roosevelt:
Ending   with the Corporations of Evil

Theodore Roosevelt was President of the United States from 1901 to 1909. He came from a family of Dutch ancestry, from the Foster's Bay branch of the family; Franklin Delano Roosevelt came from the Hyde Park branch. He was a man of one piece, dressed for his feet, a man of action straight out of the novels of Ernst Hemingway or the films of John Wayne, both of whom he preceded.

He went into the cattle business. His headquarters were on the Maltese Cross Ranch near Medora, and he built a cottage in remote country which he called Elkhorn. To harden himself, he strained his body to the limits of its endurance. He wrote to his family: "I have just arrived after spending thirteen hours on horseback. There were still some buffalo and Sioux Indians and the frontier was not yet closed. It all looked very much like a cowboy movie and ended with Theodore's tough, nobleman capturing the red-haired Finnigan and two cronies, for which he received a $50 reward. And to a local thug named Paddock who threatened to run him out of town, he sought him out and said, "I understand you have threatened to kill me on sight. I've come to see when you want to start and to let you know that if you have anything to say against me, now is the time to do it.

He returned to the East and married a girl named Edith. He wanted to have many children because he believed that "good blood" should do battle with the immigrant races, what he called "the war of the cradle". He sought action because "every man must show his worth" and, he believed, politicians should not send soldiers into battle "without knowing what a war is", so in Cuba he enlisted in the first volunteer cavalry, an elite unit that carried out commando actions. "I don't want them to be say that I'm a parlour jingoist". Theodore Roosevelt enjoyed the campaign, was the leader of the pack and led repeated attacks on San Juan Hill. He returned to the United States a public hero and became Vice President and then President. As it turns out, the 26th president of the United States had nothing to do with the lack of leadership of the demented and sober Joe Biden.

In September 1902, during a campaign tour, the president's carriage was run over by a tram: he lay on the pavement, bleeding and badly injured. His face had been badly bruised and one of his knees was so badly damaged that surgeons were on the point of amputating his leg. But he honoured his commitment and gave the planned rally. The central theme of his speech, repeated a thousand times, is of burning relevance and must be raised today, without doubt, as crucial for the survival of civilisation and the species: the need to discipline and put an end to Corporations. Theodore Roosevelt took on J. P. Morgan and his bank, he lashed out at Rockefeller and what he called the "bad trust", Standard Oil, and he took on Edward Henry Harriman mercilessly, whom he described as a "moral and social pariah"; Harriman, with Illinois Central, was dedicated to creating expectations, to buying and selling by creating fictitious value.

Standard Oil was a ruthless and predatory company. It amassed five factories and created a near monopoly, able to get discounted rates on the railways while its competitors could not. By 1879 Standard Oil controlled 90-95% of refined oil, and this fact, coupled with its new pipeline system, gave it absolute control over the railways. However, it succeeded in making the product cheaper for consumers. The barrel of oil was 0.06 a gallon and he brought it down to 0.03 a gallon. In his first phase of expansion he was able to reduce the retail price of paraffin, a by-product used in every household in the United States, by 70 per cent. Supposedly, for a liberal ideology, it was a free market process and political power could only allow it, accelerate it and remove obstacles.

Somehow, capitalism ends up benefiting consumers, is the dogma. At the beginning of the 20th century, this doctrine had been endorsed by the Supreme Court presided over by John Marshall, one of the most influential men in American history, who had made the rise of corporations possible. Marshall defined them as follows: "a corporation is an artificial, invisible, intangible being that exists in legal terms. As a mere product of law, it possesses only three qualities which are explicitly or implicitly conferred upon it by the statutes of its creation. The most important of these are immortality and, if I may say so, individuality, properties which cause a perpetual succession of persons to be regarded as an individual and to be able to act as such".

The truth is that Theodore saw far greater risks on the horizon and wanted to put a stop to them. He was not a social resentment, for he himself was wealthy, but he saw that these corporations would eventually turn against man. Today we find ourselves in a situation where 1% of the population accumulates 99% of the wealth. A fact offered by an ngo and collected by **the 2001 Nobel laureate in economics, Joseph Sitiglitz.** Let's take it for granted. Liberalism, from the Austrian school, with Friedrich Hayek, tells us that such accumulation is beneficial and good as long as it is the product of spontaneous order. And that globalisation benefits the consumer because lower costs benefit the consumer who receives cheaper products while, for example in China, it would produce a middle class which, we are told, would demand democratic reforms.

These are nothing but dogmas. Slavery in China is becoming more and more prevalent every day and is trying to spread to humanity, including the United States. As for the 1% who accumulate 99% of the Earth's wealth, let us start from Lord Acton's axiom that "power corrupts and absolute power corrupts absolutely". What we see is that the primary sector has been destroyed by subsidising fallow land and by supplier policies that stifle the small producer.

Far from benefiting the consumer, it tries to eliminate him. Let us start with Karl R. Popper's analysis of reality and its element of contrasts. We contemplate how Malthusian and eugenic doctrines have given rise to the greatest and cruelest attempt to exterminate the population and to eliminate its most minimal rights to the point of making tyrannicide and armed insurrection legitimate. The corrupt moneyed elites have unleashed on the defenceless population the greatest programmed campaign of extermination through the human-invented coronavirus and vaccine scams, in which the pharmaceutical corporations, dominated by Bill Gates, and the media corporations, bought by the Black Rock and Vanguard investment funds, dominated by a few families among which the Rockefellers and Rothschilds stand out, have participated.

They cannot be said to benefit the consumer when they try and get the most defenceless, for example the elderly and babies, to eliminate them, to kill them, as Albert Bourla, CEO of Pfizer, has boasted at the World Economic Forum. These elites are satanic, they worship satan. On the death of John Rockefeller it became known that he had installed a statue in homage to Satan and named his Manhattan skyscraper 666. And the Rothschilds are known for the Satanism of Jacob, the head of the family, as he made clear by photographing himself with the notorious satanist Marina Abramovic in front of the painting: "satan summoning his legions". Satan's goal is to eliminate the human species, God's creature.

It is imperative to disarm the enemy by taking away his wealth; this is a moral war, and battles are won when the enemy's supply lines are cut. In principle, the confiscation of assets is repugnant to the American mentality, but the growing resistance, the demos, the victory, is forbidden if the assets of the globalist companies and individuals who conspire against us are not seized. The legacy of the great Theodore Roosevelt must be urgently taken up and put into practice.

Measures to be implemented:

1.- Responsibilities for the deaths in the pandemic and the consequences of the vaccine scams. All victims should be compensated by the pharmaceutical companies and their shareholders, in cascade, with multi-million compensations.

2.- Fines should be paid by the media and social networks that have imposed the genocidal narrative and by the investment funds that have encouraged it.

3.- It will have to be seen whether the Corporations have fallen into corporatism and mercantilism, and through them and their foundations have implemented collusive and monopolistic policies, so that they have changed policies for their own benefit through subsidies and by plundering public funds, for example through the climate scam and the ecological transition. This money will have to be paid back to the state and taxpayers with high interest rates.

This is probably the most important transfer in the history of goods and it is urgent to get down to work. Either that or we succumb. And we will not succumb.

Whites as outcasts and the corruption of minors

At the end of the 19th century, a secret society of self-promotion, markedly sodomite, was formed in Cambridge, called the "twelve apostles", from which the Bloomsbury group emerged. In 1902 this sort of Freemasonry or cultural mafia elected Lyton Strachey, who led it for 30 years, and to which the economist John Keynes belonged. Lyton wrote Eminent Victorians, a World War I plea against Western values in the Anglo-Saxon world. Although Strachey said that "we are all physically too weak to be of any use", they applied the pickaxe against democratic societies and gave three of the most notorious Russian spies.

Lyton Strachey confided to Keynes that "we cannot be content with telling the truth, we must tell the whole truth, and the whole truth is the devil. It would be absurd for us to dream of the possibility of widows understanding that sentiments are good when we say in the same sentence that the best ones have a sodomite character. Our time will come in a hundred years' time.

It was and is the most corrosive attack on the sanctity of marriage, the family and the birth rate, and an unbearable supremacism, bent on imposing its criteria, corrupting minors and promoting paedophilia. The sodomites, with a few exceptions, are fervent allies of globalism, they are destructive of any adherence to the Fatherland, in themselves, in exchange for tolerating all their vices, they are a globalist movement with their infectious transnational flag.

They practise unrestricted censorship, have been fervent supporters of compulsory vaccination scams, tried to silence the voices that have cried out against genocide. Now they move, with the support of Corporations, against men and women who responsibly follow God's commandments to impose themselves through affirmative action and to dictate in schools their perversions and degradations as a a seriously distorting instrument in the maturation of children, promoting their unnatural hyper-sexualisation from the earliest childhood, promoting pederasty as a natural occurrence.

Highly symptomatic of the sodomite dictatorship is what has happened at the Disney Corporation where CEO Karey Burke, who admits she has "two queer children", supports having such characters in more Disney films and projects, demanding that at least 50 percent of all film characters be homosexual, transgender or racial minorities. This minority insanity is trying to impose itself on the majority, and when Florida Governor Ron DeSantis banned the teaching of woke ideology and transvestism to children in schools, Disney protested and said it would do everything in its power to fight and reverse the law. All he really achieved is that Florida legislators suspended Disney's privileges in Orlando, a state within the state, and that 70% of Americans have turned their backs on this large-scale industry of corruption of minors.

In fact, *City Journal*'s Christopher Rufo posted the images on Twitter, which were leaked from Disney's Reimagine Tomorrow virtual summit. He wrote: "Disney has adopted a benefits program to help employees and their minor children with 'gender affirming procedures'. This type of treatment generally includes puberty blockers, breast removal and genital surgeries for 'children who are transitioning'".

In his obsession for a world without children, for the extinction of the white race, which Satan hates for having embraced Christianity, he seeks to enter into "affirmative action", with a serious breach of the equality of all before the law, which was first proposed when in 1937 the Carnegie Foundation commissioned a report by the national socialist and Swedish Social Democratic Party ideologue Gunnar Myrdal, who in 1944 presented it under the title An American Dilemma with 1,000 pages, 250 notes and 10 appendices.In it he argued that racism ran too deep and concluded by urging the Supreme Court to apply "the spirit of the Reconstruction Amendments".

As time went on, Gunnar Myrdal produced the most corrosive attack on equality under the law, upward mobility, merit and the melting pot: the Civil Rights Act of 1964 and the Equal Employment Opportunity Commission that set in motion "affirmative action", ending the United States as we have known it, a space of freedom and opportunity. Race was replaced by ethnicity and racism was nurtured by a Hindu-like caste system, with whites occupying the undeserved place of outcasts. Affirmative action' accompanied by its first cousin 'political correctness' manifested itself in all its unrestrained nonsense and intolerance and its tendency to stifle free speech.

It is a totalitarian process of social engineering that invents new sins and anathemas such as homophobic and transphobic, changing the natural order of things, and tries to practice it in education through a general corruption of minors, of the children of normal, Christian families. Affirmative action' seeks to establish quotas for these new castes of untouchables'. It is an overwhelming and highly corrosive mischief. There is little doubt that the two souls of America cannot coexist. Either the sodomites are deported to certain areas such as San Francisco or one of the Pacific islands or there is secession of the America that is not ready to succumb.

Moral Rearmament: US Supreme Court declares abortion not a right: "Rose v Wade was eminently wrong".

In a landmark decision, the Supreme Court of the United States on 24 June 2021 has decided that abortion is neither constitutional nor a right. It thus reverses the Rose v. Wade ruling of 22 January 1973 that legalised it nationwide, holding it to be judicial sophistry that fell under the Fourteenth Amendment, which guarantees personal liberty as part of a fair trial, including a right to privacy that anti-abortion laws violated.

That meant overturning any restrictive law in any state and caused a slaughter: 30 million were performed in the 1990s at a rate of 1,600,000 a year. Another fallacy was that this number demonstrated women's acceptance, for American women, especially in some states, have never resorted to abortion, while other degenerate and highly promiscuous women have used abortion as a method of contraception with three and more abortions. The judgement states that Rose v. Wade was "eminently wrong, and in direct collision with the Constitution from the moment it was published". The Honourable Justice Samuel Alito states in the judgement: "'Roe' was remorselessly wrong from the start. Its rationale was exceptionally weak and the judgment has had disastrous consequences. And far from achieving national agreement on the abortion issue, 'Roe' and 'Casey' have stoked the debate and deepened the divide," said the drafter of the ruling, conservative Justice Samuel Alito. "It is time to abide by the Constitution and return the issue of abortion to the elected representatives of the people.

The pro-life movement, very strong in the US, gained strength as new computerised tomography techniques proved that the foetus is a human being and at a very early stage a heartbeat can be heard. Between 1987 and 1994, more than 72,000 protesters were arrested for peaceful sit-ins outside abortion clinics and many were sentenced to more than two and a half years in prison.

prison. In 1994, under pressure from the abortion lobby, Congress passed the Freedom of Access to Clinic Entrances Act, which made peaceful picketing a federal crime punishable by up to ten years in prison.

Each state will now be able to restrict abortion and an estimated 31 states have passed very restrictive laws, up to Oklahoma's total ban. These include Alabama, Arkansas, Arizona, Florida, Georgia, Idaho, Indiana, Iowa, Kentucky, Louisiana, Michigan, Mississippi, Missouri, Montana, Nebraska, North Dakota, Ohio, Oklahoma, the Carolinas, Tennessee, Texas, Utah, West Virginia, Wisconsin and Wyoming. By contrast, "Democratic" states already contemplate laws legalising infanticide, in an orgy of crime, such as California and Maryland.

The Court, in a 6-3 ruling driven by its conservative majority, upheld a Republican-backed Mississippi law banning abortion after 15 weeks. The Mississippi law had been blocked by lower courts as a violation of Supreme Court precedent. Now the justices argue that the Roe v. Wade decision was wrongly decided because the US Constitution does not specifically mention the right to abortion.

By eliminating abortion as a constitutional right, the ruling restores the ability of states to pass laws banning abortion. Twenty-six states are considered certain or likely to now ban abortion. Mississippi is among 13 states that already have so-called 'automatic trigger laws' designed to ban abortion if Roe v. Wade is overturned.

Abortion is likely to remain legal in criminal Democrat and Satanist states. Currently, more than a dozen states have laws protecting abortion rights. Numerous Republican-led states have passed various abortion restrictions in defiance of the Roe precedent in recent years.

Insane and sober Joe Biden has little choice but to oppose it, although this historic and just decision opens up hope that of the two souls of the United States, the one of good may triumph.

Justice Thomas: Supreme Court should reconsider rulings on same-sex marriage and contraception

Supreme Court Justice Clarence Thomas wrote Friday that the high court should reconsider rulings on contraception, same-sex relationships and same-sex marriage in a lone concurring opinion released Friday that overturned Roe v. Wade.

The Republican-appointed judge argued that the Supreme Court should reconsider other cases that fall under due process precedents.

"I write separately to emphasise a second, more fundamental reason why there is no abortion guarantee lurking in the Due Process Clause," Thomas wrote. "Considerable historical evidence indicates that 'due process of law' simply required executive and judicial actors to comply with statute and common law when depriving a person of life, liberty, or property."

With Friday's ruling, the "court refuses to disturb substantive due process jurisprudence in general or the application of the doctrine in other specific contexts," he also wrote (pdf), adding that cases like Griswold v. Connecticut, which give married people the right to obtain contraceptives, as well as Lawrence v. Texas, a ruling on the right to participate in a "right to participate" in the United States, have been "unsettled by the court's decision.

in a private, consensual sexual act, and Obergefell v. Hodges, the right to same-sex marriage, should be reviewed.

"I agree that 'nothing in [the Court's] opinion should be understood as calling into question precedents that do not deal with abortion,'" Thomas added, citing Justice Samuel Alito's majority opinion published Friday.

The judge argued that based on that precedent, "in future cases, we should reconsider all of this Court's substantive due process precedents, including Griswold, Lawrence and Obergefell".

The 6-3 decision upheld Mississippi's 15-week abortion ban, which clashed directly with Roe v. Wade's requirement that states allow abortion up to the point of fetal viability, around 24 weeks. The ruling also overturned the 1992 Planned Parenthood v. Casey decision that reaffirmed Roe.

"Roe was terribly wrong from the start," Alito wrote for the majority in overturning the two landmark decisions. "Their reasoning was exceptionally weak and the decision has had damaging consequences. And far from achieving national agreement on the abortion issue, Roe and Casey have inflamed the debate and deepened the divide."

"It is time to heed the Constitution and return the issue of abortion to the elected representatives of the people," he continued.

As the decision reverberated across Washington, crowds of pro-life activists, who had gathered outside the courthouse for days, erupted in cheers.

"I am ecstatic," said Emma Craig, 36, of Pro Life San Francisco. "Abortion is the greatest tragedy of our generation and in 50 years we will look back on the 50 years we have been under Roe v. Wade with shame."

The Mississippi law had been blocked by lower courts as a violation of Supreme Court precedent on abortion rights. Abortion is likely to remain legal in Democratic-led states.

Currently, more than a dozen states have laws protecting abortion rights. Numerous Republican-led states have passed various abortion restrictions in defiance of the Roe precedent in recent years.

Abortion is always Satanism

Abortion is always satanic. It is a tribute to the dark lord. Satanists exist and believe they rule the world. There is the entire Rothschild family and the Rockefeller family, in economic alliance, the two major economic powers in the universe, dominating Vanguard and Black Rock, the American Federal Reserve... The Rothschilds' Satanism is evidenced by the photograph of Marina Abramovic, a self-confessed Satanist, in front of the painting "Satan summoning his legions". John Rockefeller is known for his adherence to Satan, to whom he erected the monument illustrating these pages and called his skyscraper 666.

Other known Satanists include the British royal family and Letizia Ortiz. Bill Gates, Prince Charles, Bill Clinton... addicted to sex with minors, with Jeffrey Epstein. All those who bear the mark of the beast, the symbol of the 2030 agenda.

You don't make it in Hollywood without paying homage to Satan. There's Angelina Jolie, who at the age of 23 took part in satanic rites. Or Mel Gibson's accusations that cannibalism is practised in Hollywood and that children's blood is drunk.

A frequent one is the use in satanic rituals of abortions. University of Michigan-Flint student government president Timothy Brooks, vice president Shbeib Dabaja and chief of staff Lina Azeim wrote the letter and listed resource groups such as the Satanic Temple, the American Civil Liberties Union, Planned Parenthood and the Prismatic Life Church, an LGBT sect whose holy sacrament is sodomy.

"Political pundits and those who continue to bring to light facts that have been obfuscated by political extremists will downplay this issue by using crude reductionist concepts of pro-choice or pro-life. But the harsh reality remains that this decision, if enacted, would strike a severe blow to the foundation of the constitutional liberties enumerated by the 14th Amendment to the Constitution and the judicial review process, sadly confirming the misguided partisanship of all factions of public policy in the United States," the letter said.

"This is not simply an abortion issue. It calls into question the role our government plays in upholding the rights guaranteed to us as citizens of a free republic. Each turn of a generation faces distinct challenges that shape the path of future generations. This generation will be hindered by a struggle for the right to privacy. In a nation that was conceived by the will of the free, nothing could be more fundamental to our future than the right to choose what one does with one's own body and, on a larger scale, the right to one's privacy. While it is labelled as a partisan issue, it is the right and the responsibility to take a stand and speak out against violations of the civil liberties of millions of Americans. In fact, it is the only thing that will bring about change for the better," he continued.

EXECUTIVE STATEMENT ON THE RECENTLY RELEASED SUPREME COURT ALITO DRAFT OPINION REGARDING ROE V. WADE

On behalf of the Student Government of the University of Michigan-Flint, the Brooks-Dabaja administration stands with the many millions of American citizens to condemn the unwarranted, archaic, and reprehensible briefing brought forth by the Supreme Court, one that would overturn the landmark decisions of *Roe v. Wade* as well as *Planned Parenthood v. Casey*. In an attack on the rights to privacy and bodily autonomy, perhaps the most basic of human rights, the Court has joined in the partisan war upon the most inalienable rights granted to Americans.

Political pundits and those who continue to bring forth facts that have been obfuscated by political extremists will diminish this issue by using crude reductionist concepts of pro-choice or pro-life . But the harsh reality remains that this decision, if enacted, would deliver a crushing blow to the foundation of the constitutional freedoms enumerated by the 14th amendment to the Constitution and the process of judicial review, sadly confirming the misguided partisanship of all factions of public policy in the United States.

This is not simply an abortion issue. It calls into question the role in which our government plays in upholding the rights guaranteed to us as citizens of a free republic. Each turn of a generation is encountered with distinct challenges that shape the path of future generations to come. This generation will be encumbered by a fight for the right to privacy. In a nation that was conceived by the will of the free, nothing can be more fundamental to our future than the right to choose what one does with their own body, and on a grander scale, the right to their privacy. While labeled as a partisan issue, it is the right and responsibility of informed citizens to take a stand, to speak out against violations of the civil liberties of millions of Americans. Indeed, it is the only thing that will spark change for the better.

The University of Michigan- Flint's Student Government condemns these actions that will affect the rights of thousands of individuals, and in particular, the rights of the students we represent. Often in the wake of great injustices such as this, the need for resources by those impacted often arises. As Student Government, it is our duty to share resources that would assist students faced with the repercussions of this potential decision, as well as ways to speak out against these civil injustices. Below are resources that focus on the issues stemming from restricting access to rights guaranteed by the precedents of *Roe v. Wade* and *Planned Parenthood v. Casey*.

Resources & Donation Links:

The Reclaim Project: Reclaim Project
Donation Link: Donate – Reclaim Project
Planned Parenthood: Planned Parenthood Action Fund
The Afiya Center: The Afiya Center
Gender Justice: Gender Justice
Pro Choice America: Michigan
Center for Reproductive Rights: Center for Reproductive Rights
Planned Parenthood: Planned Parenthood | Official Site
Yellowhammer Fund: Yellowhammer Fund
The Satanic Temple: The Satanic Temple
Church of Prismatic Light: Church of Prismatic Light
ACLU: ACLU

Attest,

Timothy J. Brooks

President

Shbeib Dabaja

Vice President

Lina Azeim

Chief of Staff

Big League Politics [has reported](#) on how the Satanic Temple argues in court that the killing of babies is a religious ritual to serve their dark lord with human sacrifice:

Marina Abramovic, Princess of Asturias Laureate, with Jacob Rothschild, in front of the painting "Satan summoning his legions".

The Satanic Temple (*TST) is [challenging state-level abortion restrictions](#) by claiming that murdering and dismembering babies is part of its religious practice.*

In reality, they are arguing that states that stand up to protect life infringe on their religious freedom to perform ritual abortions.

"TST bases its assertions of exemptions from the abortion mandate on protections provided by state Religious Freedom Restoration Acts, or RFRAs, which generally prohibit the government from substantially interfering with a person's free exercise of religion," TST wrote in a press release.

The TST hopes the courts will strike down anti-abortion laws enacted at the state level to protect their right to sacrifice sacred children for their dark lord. They wrote that "religious abortions during the first trimester are exempt from state regulations that hinder access to pregnancy termination services and serve no medical purpose".

"Many states have laws that interfere with our members' ability to practice their religious beliefs. No Christian would accept a mandatory waiting period before being able to participate in Communion," said Jane Essex, who works as a reproductive rights spokesperson for TST.

"No Christian would tolerate a law that insists that state advice is necessary before someone can be baptised. Our members have a just right to religious freedom to be able to practice our rituals as well," he added.

Abortion has become a modern day sacrament for the ungodly and wicked youth of America and the world. Christians must defeat this agenda of organised evil decisively, or America and the whole world will go the way of Sodom and Gomorrah.

A direct line runs from abortion to the genocide of the vaccine scam. The indiscriminate killing of unborn babies that has taken place in the United States since the 22 January 1973 Roe vs. Wade" - 30 million heinous crimes were carried out in the 1990s - has had its perverse logic continued in the genocide that has been and continues to be carried out with the thymus vaccines, which already accounts for four times the normal mortality and the loss of between 82% and 96% of the babies of pregnant women who received the lethal injection, as well as a plague of hepatitis among the youngest children.

Filthy, satanic companies such as Microsoft or Amazon that advertise payment for the abortions of their workers, placed at the level of the worst murderers and of fragile virtue, appear implicated in the official and censorious narrative that has been carried out by the propaganda for the inoculation of the poison of the royal cobra.

This straight line between abortion and the genocide of thymus vaccines involves the same concept of population elimination and the same eugenic character.

San Francisco archbishop bans Nancy Pelosi from receiving the Body of Christ for her public pro-abortion stance

San Francisco Archbishop Salvatore Cordileone has barred U.S. House Speaker Nancy Pelosi from receiving communion for supporting abortion rights, according to a letter from the archbishopric released Friday.

Archbishop Cordileone stated in the letter that he had previously asked Pelosi to "publicly repudiate her advocacy of the 'right' to abortion or else refrain from referring to her Catholic faith in public and from receiving Holy Communion", or she would be excluded from access to this Sacrament.

"Since you have not publicly rejected your position on abortion, and continue to refer to your Catholic faith to justify your position and receiving Holy Communion, the time has come," the archbishop said. "I am therefore notifying you that you may not present yourself for Holy Communion, and that if you do, you will not be admitted to receive it, until you publicly repudiate your defence of the legitimacy of abortion and confess and receive absolution for this grave sin in the sacrament of Penance," the prelate added.

Pelosi is a so-called Catholic who has made abortion her unholy banner. According to the Catechism of the Catholic Church those who collaborate with abortion are excommunicated.

The Spike protein is a biological weapon, deliberately designed to kill.

Karen Kingston is a former Pfizer employee and a leading biotechnology analyst who has researched and published on many cutting-edge pharmaceutical topics.

Kingston argues that the alleged vaccines are actually biological weapons and that she can prove it with the FDA's own data. She also claims that the FDA investigation shows that the FDA knows that it was these biological weapons that caused all these deaths and injuries.

Kingston explains: "There were more people with Covid because of the vaccine, compared to those who received placebos; but they took 409 people out of the vaccinated group, saying they had side effects. **The side effect is illness**.

The FDA document is incriminating evidence. If Janet Woodcock (director of the FDA's Center for Drug Evaluation and Research (CDER) were to read this in the Senate, she **would be arrested immediately for grievous bodily harm and murder of American children and adults by poisoning.**

They call it side effects. When you have a meeting two months before approving this vaccine and during that meeting you list a whole list of serious chronic diseases that cause morbidity and mortality in children and adults, and you say you know it's **going to happen, it's** not a side effect. **This is an intended consequence**. This is the effect of vaccines.

The effect of vaccines is to wreak havoc on your immune system. This immune imbalance leads to heart attacks, inflammation of the heart; neurological disorders ranging from fatigue to paralysis and mental fog, rapid onset disorders, narcolepsy, death, stillbirth, birth defects and miscarriages.

They knew it was coming. In the FDA data for Pfizer, we can read: "Listen, there were more people vaccinated who got Covid. They said it was a side effect. It is not a side effect, it *IS* the effect. (...)

Most people agree that the protein spike from the Wuhan lab that was placed in the genome on 10 January is a biological weapon. If you read the FDA approval letter, what are the ingredients of the vaccines? It is synthetic mRNA code, computer-generated code generated by artificial intelligence that is injected into your body and produces, and I am quoting here verbatim, the protein spike from the complete "Wuhan -Hu-1 genome sequence". It is stated in the (FDA) approval letter that the vaccine produces a biological weapon. Data indicate that more people are vaccinated than not vaccinated with Covid-19. People say I should be an expert witness. I don't need to be an expert witness. We just need the FDA to read its own documents. "

In conclusion, Kingston said: "I think we can work with science at the molecular level to cure this, but if people don't know they're sick, millions of Americans are going to die and our children are going to be part of it. of this sacrifice. I am filled with a deep and terrible sorrow. "

4,113% more US military personnel have died since the vaccination scam!

As I have said, there is a straight line between abortion, euthanasia and the vaccine scam; the culture of death to eliminate population. But when the Armed Forces are destroyed with mandates, the surviving members have a moral obligation to arrest and prosecute the perpetrators of this genocide.

4,113 % of vaccinated US military personnel have been killed! This is the observation made by biostatistician Jessica Rose about the deaths recorded in 2021 compared to 2020. The figures on the abnormal and unusual increase in morbidity and mortality among the US military had already been reported at the beginning of 2022 and denied by the US Secretary of State for Defence, while the US military's health surveillance system is probably the best in the world. VAERS data reveal far more worrying figures than those initially announced by whistleblowers.

On 1 February[2022] , we reported on the warning issued by 3 US Army doctors and lawyers, including Thomas Renz, heard during a hearing by Senator Ron Johnson. The medical data, from the US Department of Defense and presented by the three doctors, painted a shocking picture of increased morbidity and mortality following covid injections. US military vaccinated over 96% show unprecedented adverse effects:

+ 1135% of pathological cases in 2021 compared to the five-year average previous years: outbreak of miscarriages, dazzling increase in the number of cancers, details of the data are conveyed in the article of February 1, 2010. [2022].

The Secretary of State for Defence had claimed an error in the data.

Three weeks later, we mentioned US Secretary of State for Defence Lloyd Austin's response to Senator Ron Johnson, who expressed surprise at these damning figures. The Defence Secretary responded to the senator, saying that the 2016-20 data was understated and, when corrected, is similar to the 2021 data. Peter Graves, spokesman for the Defense Health Agency's Force Oversight Division armies, told PolitiFact (subsidised media serving propaganda) via email that, in response to concerns mentioned in news reports, the division reviewed data from the *defence medical epidemiology* database (DMED) and found it to be incorrect for the years 2016-2020.

Increase in military deaths recorded in VAERS data

The Deep State lie remains the main line of defence. Dr. Theresa Long, a lieutenant colonel and one of the three whistleblowers, spoke with Dr. Pierre Kory, who is joined by biostatistician Jessica Rose in a short video posted on Twitter about post-vaccination deaths in the US military.
+4133%. The graph shown in the video is shown below:

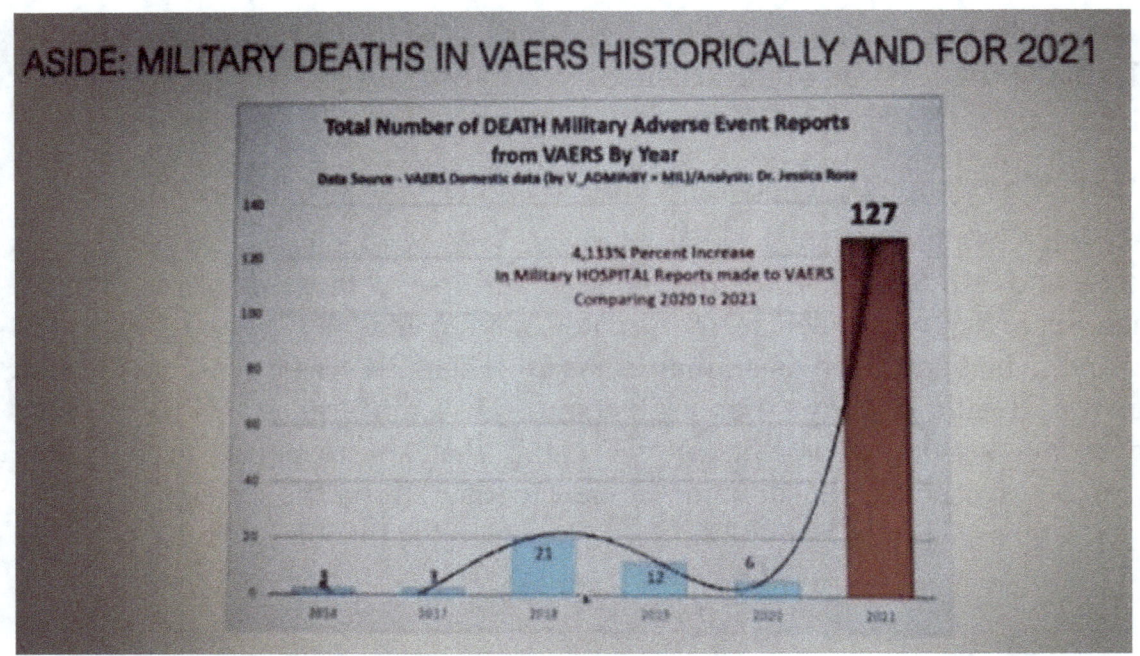

ASIDE: MILITARY DEATHS IN VAERS HISTORICALLY AND FOR 2021

The law of silence is necessary in American administration

We also learn other information, here are some selected excerpts:

Dr. Pierre Kory : "His (Theresa Long's) commanding officer told him not to testify. And she asked, is that an order? He said yes. And she said, you realize that's interference with testimony. In short, she's in the M..."

And I said Teresa, how can you still be alive, how are you still employed by the army? I mean, you should have been liquidated. She told me she was protected as a whistleblower. In fact, they can't touch her.

He told me that last year 88 soldiers at Fort Bragg *were found dead in their beds. He couldn't tell me what the numbers were the year before, but here are 88 dead soldiers at Fort Bragg. They are young, healthy soldiers...*

Jessica Rose (Biostatistics): I will tell you what the numbers are for last year because I did this analysis today on military data. So I looked at the military death entries in VAERS, there is a 4133% increase in reported military hospital deaths between 2020 and 2021.

For those who want to see the full 1:30 video between Dr. Kory and Jessica Rose, it is here. The American administration is pushing with all its weight for there to be no commission of enquiry into the issue. American soldiers will be able to continue to get sick and die without this being seen and reported, without the link to the Covid injections being highlighted.

Evil under siege: Florida Senate passes legislation to end tax privilege and special self-governing status for satanic Disney

The Florida Senate on Wednesday passed legislation to end Disney's special tax privilege and self-governing status in a 23-16 vote.

On Tuesday, Florida Governor Ron DeSantis announced that he would ask the Special Session to introduce legislation to cancel all special districts that were enacted in Florida prior to 1968 and remove exemptions from the big tech liability law.

The Florida Legislature will meet this week to consider the congressional redistricting plan for Florida for the next ten years. Governor Ron DeSantis considered getting rid of special districts enacted before 1968.

"I'm announcing today that we're extending the call for what they're going to consider this week. And yes, they will consider the congressional map, but they will also consider the termination of all the special districts that were enacted in Florida prior to 1968, and that includes the Reedy Creek Improvement District," DeSantis told a press conference.

"Disney is a guest in Florida. Today we remind you. @GovDeSantis just extended the Special Session in order to file HB3C which eliminates the Reedy Creek Improvement District, a 50-year-old special statute that exempts Disney from laws faced by ordinary Floridians," tweeted Rep. Fine.

Today, Florida lawmakers passed legislation ending Disney's tax privilege, self-governance power and special exemption status. The new bill now heads to the House.

Boycott Disney!

& All Products!

In a truly pathetic display of gross capitulation to the forces of evil ruling the Western world at this moment, Walt Disney Company CEO Bob Chapek apologised to Cult of LGBT for allegedly not promoting *enough* gender and sexual perversion in children.

In a video statement to the LGBT "community" (*see below*), Chapek was saddened by the failure to prepare children to the level required to cater to gays, lesbians, transgender and others who identify with something other than the normal man and woman.

NEW: Disney CEO Bob Chapek grovels, apologizes, and pledges to "be a better ally for the LGBTQ+ community." He delegated the company's moral authority to the "LGBTQIA+ Advisory Council" and now those internal activists have taken him as an ideological hostage. pic.twitter.com/efOSOmb47a

- Christopher F. Rufo (@realchrisrufo) April 7, 2022

"By now, I hope you have all read my most recent note in which I pledge to be a better ally to the LGBTQ+ community, apologise for not being the ally you needed me to be, and commit to ensuring that our company lives up to its values," Chapek told his virtual audience.

"I wanted to say every word. And that is what we are here to talk about today. I know we have work to do and that work starts with listening. I'm glad that the

I listened to the LGBTQ+ employee panel today, and I hope that the voices I heard over the last few weeks have impacted them as much as they have me".

Supreme Court rules Americans have right to bear arms in public

The US Supreme Court issued an unusual decision upholding constitutional gun rights, ruling 6-3 that Americans have the right to bear arms outside the home and in public, in a major victory for Second Amendment advocates. The case stems from a lawsuit filed by the New York State Rifle and Pistol Association against the state. The lawsuit argued that the restriction made it nearly impossible to obtain a lawful carry permit and turned the Second Amendment into a privilege rather than a right. The ruling will affect other states with similar laws, including California, Delaware, Hawaii, Maryland, Massachusetts, New Jersey and Rhode Island.

The US Supreme Court on Thursday issued a rare decision involving constitutional gun rights and ruled that Americans have the right to bear arms outside the home and in public, in a major victory for Second Amendment advocates.

The high court voted 6-3 to strike down a New York law that said gun owners must prove the need to carry firearms outside the home.

The court split along ideological lines, with the six conservative justices voting against the New York law and the three progressive justices voting to uphold the gun safety statute.

Writing for the majority, Associate Justice Clarence Thomas said the New York law goes too far in restricting the legal possession of firearms and said it violates the Second Amendment of the US Constitution.

"Because New York State issues common carrier licenses only when an applicant demonstrates a special need for self-defense, we conclude that the state's licensing regime violates the Constitution," Thomas wrote in the ruling.

Conservative justices Samuel Alito and Amy Coney Barrett wrote concurring opinions and Justice Stephen Breyer, who is retiring at the end of the current term, wrote a dissenting opinion.

A clear defence of freedom, of self-defence, also against the arbitrariness and oppression of the government itself.

Supreme Court rules that praying in public is freedom of expression

The Supreme Court issued a ruling Monday upholding the First Amendment right to free speech with respect to prayer. The Court ruled in favour of a high school football coach who was told he should not pray on the field after the game in the case of *Kennedy v. Bremerton School District.*

The 6-3 ruling found that the school district in 2015 violated the coach's free speech rights when it banned him from praying on the field, and that coach subsequently lost his job over the matter. The majority opinion was written by Justice Neil Gorsuch, who was joined by Chief Justice Roberts, along with Justices Clarence Thomas, Samuel Alito and Amy Coney Barrett. Justice Brett Kavanaugh joined the opinion, except for one section.

Coach Joseph Kennedy had lost his coaching job because he would kneel at midfield after games to offer a prayer, usually for about 30 seconds. The firing was because the Bremerton school district believed that allowing Kennedy to pray would indicate support for his religious beliefs. However, Gorsuch wrote: "That reasoning was flawed. Both the free exercise and free speech clauses of the First Amendment protect speech like Mr. Kennedy's." While Kennedy initially offered the prayer on his own, over time, student players joined him. When the athletes asked if they could join him, Kennedy told them, "This is a free country, you can do whatever you want. And so they did. Kennedy served at the school for seven years before there were any problems or complaints with his orations on the field or in the locker room, which had been part of the school culture.The letter to Kennedy included statements from the school that Kennedy had violated the "Establishment Clause." Gorsuch writes that "Nor does a proper understanding of the Amendment's Establishment Clause require the government to single out private religious speech for special disapproval. The Constitution and the best of our traditions counsel mutual respect and tolerance, not censorship and suppression, for religious and nonreligious". equal viewpoints".After Kennedy received the letter, he complied with its terms, which

These included no longer referring to his religious beliefs in motivational speeches, no longer offering prayers in the locker room and giving up midfield, post-game prayers. For Kennedy, however, this became too difficult and he felt he had "broken his commitment to God" by abandoning the practice. He objected to the school for this restriction and asked that he be allowed to offer his own prayer. The school refused to compromise, saying that Kennedy did not appear to endorse prayer while on duty as a coach paid by the school district. Kennedy continued to pray, often waiting until the players were otherwise occupied or off the field. But the players continued to join him in prayer. The school wanted Kennedy to hide his faith, but the court ruled that this was a violation.

The awakening of the "torch and pitchfork" days and the genocide executions, of children

Woe to the criminals and genocidaires, the day is coming soon when they will pay for their horrible deeds! The days of torches and gibbets are going to take place, sooner rather than later. The guillotines and gallows are being organised and the wrath of the people will be unstoppable, and it will be merciless in a way that they have not been merciless, first of all, by pursuing the greatest death toll among the elderly and then by spreading the death toll through all age groups, even to pregnant women and the most tender babies, who are now suffering from a plague of hepatitis or dying of sudden death. The world has woken up and justice for the masterminds and hired killers of the carnage is very close at hand.

Anthony Fauci.

Canada, which seemed to be imprisoned by the devil and headed straight for slavery, woke up with the heroic truckers, thanks and praise beyond measure for their example of heroism. And the United States has woken up, where in 25 states the patriots are in charge, who are seriously confronted with the globalists, and they gnash their teeth at the lies of Bill Gates and Anthony Fauci. CNN, Disney, Meta and Netflix are falling. Sportfy will not renew the agreement to continue sharing the Obama podcasts. We must not be blind and see the signs that many things are happening, all of them positive.

The United States is polarised. The truth is known, it is known and it is outrageous. In the USA, where the death rate has risen by 1,100% in the Armed Forces and is expected to rise to 5,000%, where the black population is being decimated, where human sacrifices to the devil have been inflicted on babies, there is an independent media reporting the truth, healthcare is not state-run so most doctors have rebelled against the disgusting lie. There, the 1,538 adverse or perverse effects of Pfizer's lethal injection reported to the FDA are public knowledge, and the FDA has had to make them public by order of a heroic federal judge in Texas. There it is already known that the damned lethal injections have many similarities with the venom of the king cobra and that the coronavirus was "invented" and patented by Moderna.

There in the United States and Canada the genocidal psychopath Bill Gates cannot set foot on the street because in Vancouver, the crippled fucker, has been surrounded by the crowd shouting "arrest Gates immediately", at the cowardice of the malformed character. This is where globalism began and where it will end in a globalist bloodbath. The November elections are looking decisive, with an insane and criminally insane Joe Biden at an all-time low in terms of approval ratings, and the electoral fraud already evident.

for all, with their globalist supporters falling apart. This election will mark a turning point in America's moral rearmament and accountability for the genocide perpetrated by the satanic globalists and the diabolical Democrat party.

Then the wave of salvation and justice will come to Europe, unstoppable, liberating; to Spain, with the government and the cacicato before justice. Glorious days of torches and pitchforks will illuminate the darkness in which the old continent is plunged.